D0064902

CARING
for Caring

CARING
for Caring

An Enriching, Kindhearted, Ethical Journey with Our Elders

Jane Edwards

CARING FOR CARING
AN ENRICHING, KINDHEARTED, ETHICAL
JOURNEY WITH OUR ELDERS

iUniverse books may be ordered through booksellers or by contacting:

iUniverse
1663 Liberty Drive
Bloomington, IN 47403
www.iuniverse.com
1-800-Authors (1-800-288-4677)

ISBN: 978-1-4917-9402-9 (sc)
ISBN: 978-1-4917-9750-1 (hc)
ISBN: 978-1-4917-9401-2 (e)

Library of Congress Control Number: 2016907466

Print information available on the last page.

iUniverse rev. date: 7/14/2016

For my grandchildren, Tatum, Micah, and Isaac,
who encouraged me and laughed with me.

Drawing by Tatum, age nine

For my dear friend Margaret Lockwood,
who inspires me in all ways.

Contents

Acknowledgments

Zen tangle by Isaac, age nine

Thanks to those people who have helped and encouraged me along the way. It is a privilege to hold you in my heart.

To Suzanne Seller, who lifted me up and enabled me to finish this work.

To Dianne Souvaine, who has always encouraged me.

Thanks to my friend Linda Hoey, who started doing the rough drafts eons ago via e-mail. Linda encouraged me and gave me a sense that I really did have something important to say.

My kudos and thanks to my coworkers, who are too many to name. You gave your loyalty to push respectful care forward. You helped to grow Caring for Caring by your insistence on walking the kindest path with our elders.

To the elders whose stories are told here posthumously,

thank you for being the greatest people on earth; you are now saints in heaven.

Thank you to my dear, dear family, who helped me and pushed me forward with note cards and words of encouragement: Alex, Micah, Tatum, Isaac, Eve, and Arnold.

To everyone who enquired about my progress over many years, thank you.

I also extend my gratitude to all my readers, from those who hold this book in their hands now to those who helped proofread the many drafts of the work.

I send gratitude to my pastor, Anne Deneen, whose graciousness and holy walk inspire me.

Gratitude also goes to Claire MacMaster, who guided me to Renee Nicholls, my copyeditor and collaborator, who then worked her magic and saw that this book was more than I could have made it alone. Thank you, dear Renee.

Special gratitude to Claire MacMaster, who saved the project in the end phase with her knowledge and many talents, not to mention her friendship.

My dream group has helped me blossom. Thank you, Joan, Jan, Peggy, Bev, Linda, Helen, and Liz.

Lastly, I send my gratitude and praise to God, who blessed this effort.

Introduction

It was always about the elders—my life, that is.

I grew up in a large farmhouse that housed my immediate family of four, two grandmothers, and oftentimes a great-aunt. I have no idea how my mother managed, but she did a masterful job of overseeing a small farm with my dad, working full-time as a registered nurse, and supervising our diverse family, which often included two young cousins.

This complex lifestyle raised in me a rich respect for my elders, which has carried me along from early childhood through adulthood. I was taught to honor my elders and to accommodate their needs cheerfully, regardless of what I thought about any requests. As a result, I find myself able to this day to respect and love our elders for who they are without needing to have an agenda of improvement.

I hope that this book will raise in you a new understanding of our elders, whether they be relatives or just folks who need a little attention. It is my dearest wish that the reflections, stories, and suggestions will broaden the way in which you treat the elders who cross your path and inspire you to support their desire to remain in their own homes.

My Journey to Caring for Elders

After growing up on the farm, I went to college at Colby Junior College in New London, New Hampshire, to study liberal arts, which was the thing to do in the 1950s. After graduation I was slated to go to nurses' training, but an invitation from a friend to come and live with her in New York City won out. I moved to New York City, where I worked for *Sports Illustrated* and *New York Magazine* in its rebirth from the *New York Herald Tribune*. Yet, even at that time, I always kept an eye out for the elders in my apartment building.

In the early 1970s, my husband and I moved to New Jersey. There we raised our two children, Alexandria and Arnold, and I created a mission that was based out of my church, the First Presbyterian Church of Boonton, New Jersey, to keep local elders in their own homes. I saw this as a deacon's call. The children were happy to help deliver holiday meals on our best china and never complained that our own holiday meals were warmed up after all the deliveries were done.

By the time I moved to Massachusetts in the early nineties, I was a single mom. My children were in college in the Boston area, and I was without a career. I thought I should look for work in a field in which I had some understanding—caring for (and respecting) our elders.

As I researched my options, I observed how things

were going for our elders north of Boston, and I did not like what I saw. In most of the facilities I visited, the needs of the elders were not considered the top priority. With in-home care, I found most workers to be rude and disrespectful; they made no effort to draw out the elders. Televisions were always blaring. To me, this was pretty much unacceptable all the way around. I decided to create my own agency to deliver respectful, honoring, and empowering care to seniors in my area. I would make an all-out effort to keep people at home.

I invited a few people to join me as subcontractors. I reviewed my philosophy with them, and they agreed to deliver care my way. Our first clients were a husband and wife who needed assistance in order to remain in their home. Working as a team, with grace and love, we gave these elders the support they needed to live independently, including home-cooked meals, rides to doctors' appointments, help with absentee ballots, and even music. The hours we spent with this couple were so rewarding. We loved them, and we quickly learned that the focus of compassionate elder care should be to ask seniors what they want instead of dictating what they need. We recognized that the elders, of course, still had opinions, and we honored those opinions.

Our positive reputation quickly spread around town, and we gained other elders as clients. Mostly our hours are distributed two hours here and two hours there—but to this day, my team and I love it, and we are happy going out the door to work each morning. Cases do grow as needs increase for our clients, but even in cases where our time is limited to two-hour shifts, we find that we can work miracles in those two hours. The stories in this volume will testify to that.

The agency's name is Caring for Caring, a name given to me by my friend Mike Parillo, who said it was an apt description of our work. Sadly, Mike died shortly thereafter, but I named the agency as a tribute to him. This name and the agency are registered with the town of Rockport, Massachusetts. The agency has grown over twenty-two years simply by word of mouth—no advertising whatsoever (although I did just give in to printing calling cards in 2014). To date, we have worked with more than 120 families. We charge an hourly rate that is commensurate with other agencies. For my role as manager, I take a very small percentage of the subcontracting workers' pay to cover agency expenses, always keeping in mind the need for all to earn a living wage.

To my way of thinking, nothing is more important than recognizing that the world of our elders is full of wonder, rich humor, and intuitiveness. I have learned that the private world of our elders is filled with wisdom for our age. It is Caring for Caring's privilege and responsibility to explore these rich attributes and to validate the elders as we care for them. We bring to them a smidge of joy, a pleasant ambiance, good medical care, relief of worries, and the all-important *fun!*

Over the years, I have personally experienced a spiritual and emotional rotation that has come full circle, and I no longer worry about my future, despite my limited finances. I have learned to do what is necessary in a given day and give no emotional weight to what the future holds. I see this as a calling from God. I am sure that being unworried is a gift of grace.

This book begins with a series of reflections that explain our philosophy as caregivers. It also includes a collection of fascinating stories about some of the elders who were able to remain in their homes thanks to the support they received from their families and my staff of coworkers—to whom both the elders and I are greatly indebted. I have been journaling about my clients for twenty-two years. This book is the result of this enriching daily habit.

It is my wish that you, dear readers, will be enlightened by our philosophy and that our experiences, stories, and suggestions will enrich your own journey when the time comes for you to consider how to help the elders in your life remain as independent—and cherished—as possible.

Part 1: Reflections

The following reflections on the philosophy of Caring for Caring are put forth to help explain why Caring for Caring has been successful for twenty-two years.

In these reflections, I use first-person narration and the word *I* for simplicity's sake, but in practice, the staff members at Caring for Caring work as a close-knit team.

It is my hope that readers will be inspired by our approach and apply our positive philosophy to their own situations with their elders.

1. Family Dynamics

You don't choose your family.
They are God's gift to you, as you are to them.

—Desmond Tutu

Before a client comes under our care, I first go and meet the family. During the initial visit, I pay special attention to family dynamics. Each family member and friend will become part of the caregiving team.

Each person in the family comes with his or her own set of realities. I listen carefully, try to be understanding, and consider each person's input. At this point, I put aside my personal shyness to adopt the role of gentle advocate for the client.

As I form an idea of what will be most beneficial to the client, my initial goal is to help the family resolve any issues in the kindest way so that we can move forward on our journey together. I am not the resolution; I am simply a gentle guide.

During the initial meeting, I try to smooth the raw edges for family or friends who are anxious. By the end of the meeting, we have set goals and formed plans. If families and caregivers can work together in harmony, then clients will benefit the most, and all parties will be confident that the cherished elders are receiving the full attention and care they deserve.

2. Perspective

*The best way to find yourself is to lose yourself
in the service of others.*

—*Mahatma Gandhi*

When members of our Caring for Caring team show up at the door of a client's house, they leave all their own issues on the doorstep.

The shift is never about my team; it is all about the client.

3. Preserving Wisdom

Wisdom is not bought.

—*Anonymous*

When we relegate our wisdom-rich elders to the utter and demeaning borders of our society, we are actually cutting ourselves off from wisdom that comes to those who are ripening into old age.

When we are young, it is hard for us to fathom that wisdom exists in the outer regions of age. We conclude that we pretty much know all that we need to know, and we don't even recognize that there *is* more wisdom out there in the world.

Yet ignoring the wisdom of our seniors is just one more thing that is countercultural in our society. Only when we begin to honor, respect, and acknowledge the wisdom that is housed in our elders—and to respect and empower them as complete beings with the right to live their lives as independently as possible—will our society finally benefit from their repositories of great knowledge and common sense.

4. Priceless Pearls

And upon finding one pearl of great value,
he went and sold all that he had and bought it.
—Matthew 13:46

"Our elders" is an expression of great respect in many societies. Elders are considered to be like the pearl of great price in Matthew 13:46. With each new day, my experiences remind me that our elders are truly invaluable. As a society, we just need to learn to treat them as such.

5. Planning Last Moments

"Life has to end," she said. "Love doesn't."
—*Mitch Albom*, The Five People You Meet in Heaven

Dying, which is a part of living, is a topic that should be up for discussion. I do bring it up with our elders so that they know what is available and what their choices are. Yet sometimes family members are appalled that I even mention it. Do they think it is better to be silent and pretend nothing is happening?

In our society we do not discuss death. We pretty much don't even use the word *dead*. We use "pass on" or "go home to the Lord." In most of our communications, we do not discuss death or the many issues around it.

However, everyone should have a choice, and everyone's choice should be honored. At the very least, we should discuss what our elder's wishes are. Does he want to have cremation, a coffin burial, a pine-box burial, or some other arrangement? Does she wish to have hospice care at the end of her life? Does he or she wish to have a DNR (do not resuscitate) order?

All adult family members, regardless of health and age, should choose health care proxies who will represent them if there is a time when they can't communicate their own wishes. These wishes should be communicated with the health care proxies in advance, written down, and stored in a place that is readily available if the time comes when they are needed. Even if specific wishes aren't currently legal in certain states, it is worth noting them in case the laws change down the road. These steps are particularly important as elders begin to navigate the rocky path of declining health.

As families, we tend to let the subject of death go unmentioned—as if it could be bypassed. However, it cannot be ignored. We all die at some point, and we owe it to our elders to give them the opportunity to sculpt the way they wish to be cared for and how they want their bodies treated after death.

6. Two Steps beyond the Physical

Too often we underestimate the power of a touch, a smile, a kind word, a listening ear, an honest compliment, or the smallest act of caring, all of which have the potential to turn a life around.
—Leo Buscaglia

In their attempts to do what seems best for their loved ones, some families overlook their elders' emotional and spiritual needs and instead focus exclusively on physical accommodations.

Yet, devoting attention to physical safety is not enough. The immense and crucial areas of emotional and spiritual needs continue throughout life, and they frequently serve as the core of our elders' growth and happiness. As we look at the broad picture and make our plans for senior care, it is essential to note that just because elders may now be diminished physically or mentally, it does not mean they do not have the same kinds of emotional and spiritual needs as they used to have—they may have even more.

7. Establishing Trust

No soul is desolate as long as there is a human being
for whom it can feel trust and reverence.

—*T. S. Eliot*

During the upheaval that often accompanies changes to an elder's independent status, our loved ones may need to be reminded of who they really are. To establish trust and to help rekindle the elder's sense of self, I always begin by engaging the client in conversation. I start with the weather or introduce myself and tell a story. Often it takes several visits and "chats" before the elder will respond at all.

Sometimes the initial reticence is due to dementia, and sometimes it is due to the diminishment the elder has experienced along the way. For instance, when elders enter a facility such as a clinic for physical rehabilitation, they rarely maintain a good self-image and usually lose contact with their real selves. I do not fault the workers at these facilities, but it is a fact that the environment itself tends to cause a shutdown.

Sometimes people are just shy, which can be a challenge for me. However, given time, I always have great success creating positive relationships once I have gained the elder's trust. Then, as our mutual feelings of trust blossom into open, friendly, and respectful communication, we are on the happy road to reestablishing the senior in a place of self-respect and growth.

8. Joyful Moments

You don't stop laughing when you grow old,
you grow old when you stop laughing.
—George Bernard Shaw

It has been my sad experience to observe that pleasure is often not one of the considerations when families and friends begin to think about care for a particular elder.

It is a familiar story for me. The families approach me and ask, "How can we make our loved one physically safe?" There are, of course, important measures we can take to facilitate safety for our elders: tub seats, grab bars in helpful places, fortified railings, rug anchors, and so forth. However, while the safety issue is essential, it should not interfere with such enjoyment as the elder desires and is able to partake in.

When I first meet an elder who is in need of some assistance, I very carefully suggest that we plan to go beyond *needs* so that we may consider *wants* as well. To achieve this, I start out by asking what is most enjoyable for the elder. I find that "What gives you pleasure?" is a good place to start. If he or she is reticent, I ask about chocolate. That usually gets something going.

9. Elder Sight Line

You never really understand a person until you
consider things from his point of view—
until you climb into his skin and walk around in it.
　　　　　　—*Harper Lee*, To Kill a Mockingbird

Some time ago, while listening to National Public Radio, I was fascinated by a segment about Gretchen Berland, a physician who had been awarded a MacArthur award for the documentaries she created by giving cameras and recording devices to interns, patients with disabilities, and cancer patients.[1] The perspective of these documentaries particularly intrigued me, because it showed each situation from the inside out.

In my work, I try to get inside my clients' world to see what they are experiencing. For instance, I sometimes sit in the client's favorite chair so I can see what the world looks like from that individual's perspective. I try to become the client's camera. This helps me identify exactly what's going on—and what needs to be fine-tuned.

1　Also see www.washingtonpost.com/wp-dyn/articles/A55569-2004Sep27.html.

10. A Different Kind of Exile

*Look into your own heart, discover what it is that gives
you pain, and then refuse, under any circumstances
whatsoever, to inflict that pain on anybody else.*

—Karen Armstrong

Exile is a word that brings a stream of dark sadness to the heart. Think of exile and what feelings it raises up in all of us: gloom and despair.

My clients are all striving to avoid what many view (often correctly) as the final exile: a move to a nursing home. I have worked with our elders for forty-five years, and I can assert that exile is what they feel when they have been sent to a nursing home. This is a step that involves a disorientating move, unknown ways, and many strangers.

There are several steps that families can take to help keep elders out of nursing homes. The stories and suggestions throughout this book are intended to support their journeys to accomplish this through at-home care. The following list of resources may also help.

+ David Fisher, MD, *How to Keep Mom (and Yourself) Out of a Nursing Home: Seven Keys to Keeping Your Independence* (Boston, David Fisher, MD, LLC, 2010).

* Atul Gawande, MD, *Being Mortal: Medicine and What Matters in the End* (New York, Henry Holt and Company, LLC, 2014).
* Maggie Callanan and Patricia Kelley, *Final Gifts: Understanding the Special Awareness, Needs, and Communications of the Dying* (NYC, Bantam Books, Simon & Schuster, 2011).
* Joanne Koenig Coste, *Learning to Speak Alzheimer's: A Groundbreaking Approach for Everyone Dealing with the Disease* (Boston, Mariner Books, Houghton Mifflin Harcourt Co., 1999).
* William H. Thomas, MD, *What Are Old People For? How Elders Will Save the World* (Boxborough, Ma., VanderWyk and Burnham, 2004)
* Robert F. Bornstein, PhD, and Mary A. Languirand, PhD, *When Someone You Love Needs Nursing Home, Assisted Living, or In-Home Care* (New York, Harper Collins, 2009).

11. Holding On to the Webbing

A thousand fibers connect us with our fellow men.
—*Herman Melville*

Mulling over the treatment of evacuees after Hurricane Katrina, I found myself unsurprised at the way people were shuffled around with little or no concern for their own personal wishes. Sadly, our society often treats elders in the same way, shuffling them off to nursing homes regardless of their position and ability to choose.

When we determine the best way to care for our elders during their final years, it is important to consider the labyrinth of webbing that they experience in their own communities. As we make plans to help them remain at home, we must also take steps to keep them connected, help them survive, and add the vital opportunity for growth in their lives. Resources like *www.eldercare.gov* (phone 800-677-1116) can help to locate available support in the senior's area for issues such as

+ home-delivered meals,
+ rides to doctor appointments,
+ assistance with light chores,
+ home repairs and modification, and
+ ways elders can stay connected to the community.

Please take a hard look at what is offered. Consider whether it measures to the highest standards of honor and respect. When you are seeking help, notice whether the person on the other end of the line is just doing a job or really has the elder's best interest at heart. When you have cleared the first level, pay the same attention to each additional level of care that is placed before you for consideration.

12. Confinement with Honor

Death is not extinguishing the light; it is putting
out the lamp because the dawn has come.
—Rabindranath Tagore

The final moments of bedside care are as complex as the entire universe.

Most people in our culture think the primary tasks in senior care involve tending to cleanliness and physical safety. Not so, I say. Rather, these undertakings are miniscule compared to the depth of supporting the departure of a dying elder. If my client is to transition holistically from this life to the next, I must help ensure that an intricate, beautiful, and mysterious journey is begun.

I take tender care of details as the end approaches. I keep everything needed (medicine, lip balm, ice chips, and so forth) right within my reach so that I do not have to leave the bedside. I sit quietly, but I also make sure that no one whispers in the background. Sometimes it causes the bedridden person to wonder what's being said and what is going to happen next. Whispering is disquieting.

As the caregiver, I am presented with myriad opportunities to help create a sense of empowerment and value to an elder. In these moments, I tell seniors that they are wonderful and of great value. If I know their faith background, I quote them verses that are empowering.

Caring involves honoring every cell of the person before me. I lock eyes and listen carefully to this person. I respect and honor this person. I watch the rich completion of a life unfold before me. Sometimes the moment of terminal lucidity happens. The client senior says a word of encouragement to those gathered around the bed or smiles brightly at a loved one. At this point, the elder's breathing has usually become irregular and noisy, although it may be quieted by the administration of medicine. At this stage of the journey, I try as best I can to tell those who have gathered what is happening. When everything is calm, the senior drifts away into the next world and simply stops breathing. It is sometimes difficult to know which has happened first.

13. A Dream for Today

The dream is the small hidden door in the deepest
and most intimate sanctum of the soul …
                                        —*Carl Gustav Jung*

As a seeker of wisdom, I try to remember my dreams. When I do remember, I write them down. I consider my dreams to be all my own creation and a probe into my psyche.

The rewards for delving into dreams can be amazing and abundantly rich. For example, I experienced pure joy from the dream recorded below.

> *Joan is moving to a lovely place. She has lots of land. Beautiful, waist-high rabbit hutches are there for Joan's many beloved bunnies. Each cage has high piles of bright orange carrots and leafy green lettuces for all the bunnies.*

> *Joan and I are happy.*

This dream came to me just before Joan's death. Here, on the outside of the dream, I am smiling inside and out.

14. Adaptable Caring

Thou wilt support us both when little
And even to grey hairs.
　　　　　—Saint Augustine (AD 354–430)

There are some things that are basic to starting work with a new client. My team and I have all agreed that it is essential to handle new situations in the following ways.

+ When we begin to work with a new elder, we say to ourselves, "This is my mother" or "This is my father." We proceed with this level of care and respect in mind.

+ We remember that each client has new and different needs from anyone we have worked with in the past. We think, "I can help" and "There can be a happy outcome."

+ When we evaluate the new client's situation, we remember that things have likely been this way for a long, long time. Any suggestions we might wish to make, or any changes the elders agree to, should be implemented as gradually as possible. For example, if the elder's nails are dirty, I don't approach the subject on my first visit. Those nails have been that way a long time. It's better to skip the nails and concentrate on companionship until a trust is established. My coworkers are not judged by what they accomplish or how fast they accomplish it. This gives them space to relax and form a trust foundation.

+ Whether this elder is new to us or we are becoming more familiar with this person, we don't move anything in the house. If we dust, we lift items straight up, dust, and place them back exactly as they were. If something represents imminent danger, we explain the situation and ask permission to move it to eliminate the hazard.

+ Whatever we do, we think, "How will this affect the client?" Chances are pretty good that our elders have already been diminished unintentionally, and we need to make sure we don't do anything to further that diminishment.

I recall a case in which Caring for Caring had been on duty for nearly a year with ninety-four-year-old Esther. Then the family found someone to live in, and we worked only occasionally to give respite to the live-in worker. When I first met with the live-in worker, I explained my theory about not moving things, explaining how it could disorient elders. However, when I returned to Esther's house, the worker was so proud of the job she had done. She had completely cleaned and revamped the kitchen.

Up until this time, Esther had always been able to

go to the kitchen and get herself a snack. (This snack procurement happened more often than you would believe in a twenty-four-hour time frame.) Unfortunately, after the cleaning Esther never used the kitchen again. In essence, it was no longer her kitchen.

As noted, when we approach a client's house, we leave our own troubles outside the door. But each time we enter the house we must also examine our good intentions—and the potential results—very carefully before we put them into action. The bottom line is that the elders must always come first. Throughout our work, we strive to remain flexible and understanding. When we are in doubt, we check in with one another and work together to determine the best steps to take.

15. Tweaking Nutrition

I scream, you scream, we all scream for ice cream.
—*Anonymous*

When we begin working with a new client, we check out the kitchen to see what is in the freezer and the refrigerator. We are generally horrified. It is usually smelly in there, and the food is almost old enough to appear on *Antiques Roadshow*. We address this situation very slowly, generally by bringing dinner with us on the first shift. Then the elder gets involved, and we are off and running toward at least a small change toward better nutrition.

It is unfortunate that the food that is marketed via advertising to our elders is heavy on salt and sugar, which seniors' taste buds also seem to steer them toward. In particular, frozen dinners—even vegetable blends—are often rich with many things you would be hard pressed to pronounce.

To address this, whenever we have some control over shopping and meal preparation, we slowly try to reduce the elders' salt and sugar intake without talking it up too much. We often make homemade dishes and inquire about preferences. Nutrition is a challenge, but we rise up to it. We talk a lot about food among ourselves.

Sometimes the dietary restrictions provided by

the senior's medical team aren't easy to implement. I remember one man who loved fresh tomatoes but felt that they needed salt. He had a heart condition, so we had weaned him off most salt, but we were able to get the green light from his physical team to offer the salt shaker with fresh tomatoes.

Overall, we try to follow the various diets people are on, but we are in the business of bringing joy to the elders, so if the medical requirements aren't too severe, we occasionally cheat a little. We consider each client's food separately and arrange meals attractively to turn appetites on. The bottom line is that we want mealtime to be especially pleasant and enjoyable, to keep the elders from simply deciding not to eat much at all.

We often join our elders for lunch or dinner. We are always well received, and the seniors consume more vegetables this way.

The National Institute of Health informs us on its web page that older adults should limit their sodium intake to 1,500 milligrams; this helps to keep blood pressure under control and can lower the risk of heart disease, stroke, congestive heart failure, and kidney disease. NIH also tells us to control calorie intake by limiting foods and drinks that are high in added sugar.

16. From Hopelessness to Hope

Life's most persistent and urgent question is
"What are you doing for others?"
—Martin Luther King Jr.

As I wrote the preface to this book, I recalled a wonderful, intuitive client named Isabel, whose life was rich and full.

On the day that she was diagnosed with Alzheimer's disease, she experienced the typical feelings of hopelessness that patients go through when their friends, family, and even the doctor suddenly seem to shut down. Initially, Isabel felt diminished beyond description. Her husband was in a turmoil of rage and denial. A veil of hopelessness dropped down over husband and wife.

That day, when Isabel asked the doctor a series of questions—some of them more than once—he lost his temper and shouted at her, "You have Alzheimer's, and there is nothing you can do about it!"

Fortunately, my experiences with the clients of Caring for Caring have clearly shown otherwise. In fact, one of the most essential ways we can support our seniors is simply to remain open to possibilities. As the following stories show, even when dementia is present, or other challenges occur, all is *not* hopeless. In fact, there are many, many things we can do about it.

Part 2: Journey Stories

Draw your chair up close to the precipice and I'll tell you a story.
—*F. Scott Fitzgerald*, Notebooks

Now on to some of the true stories that show the philosophy of Caring for Caring playing out for our elders. Hopefully they will give you joy and laughter as you read through them. I am sharing some of these stories simply because they are fun, but I've included others to offer you ideas on how to care for and protect your elders when the time comes around for you to be the caregiver and support their desire for independent living.

1. In the Beginning

Tea is liquid wisdom.

—*Anonymous*

Kathleen and Bruce were an older couple who lived in Boonton, New Jersey, the town next to ours when we lived in that state. They were members of our church. Kathleen was crippled by rheumatoid arthritis, and she was confined to a wheelchair. She had maintained her upper body strength so that she could transfer from her wheelchair to her hospital bed with little assistance from Bruce. The hospital bed was in the living room near the front door. Kathleen held on to her control of her household from that position.

I went for tea twice a week, and we always gathered around a card table for tea and the cookies that I would bring from a bakery. Kathleen hesitated to talk about the past, because their son had died while at college. They had received a call that he was sick, but when they'd arrived on the campus, he had already been dead. Hearing their story reminded me that we just don't know what others suffer, which is a good reason to be patient and kind to all we meet along the way. At any rate, we often enjoyed our tea as silently as mice.

One day an idea popped into my head, and I asked Kathleen whether she had favorite cookies for which she had recipes. She began to reminisce about the ones she and Bruce had loved the best. We got out the recipe box, and she ran her fingers over the tops of the cards and randomly pulled some "best" cookie recipes from the collection.

I began to make those cookies and bring them to our teatimes. This led us to talking about the past, even the painful parts. Bruce, though shy, joined in as he broke each cookie into segments to enjoy one piece at a time—a habit we teased him about mercilessly as we reminded him that most people simply bit their cookies. He never seemed to mind.

Kathleen and Bruce had an adult daughter who lived in the west and was very attentive to their needs. When she visited, that made four of us sitting around the card table, often smiling and not saying a word as we bit and Bruce broke.

One day Bruce was out walking in town when he fell and broke his hip. There arose an immediate clatter that the couple would need to go to a nursing home.

"Absolutely not!" I said. A friend named Ann Peck took turns with me sleeping over with Kathleen while Bruce was in the hospital, and we worked alongside other church members to see to Kathleen's needs.

When Bruce was rehabilitated, the discussion of a nursing home came up again. Again I said, "Absolutely not!" Then I suggested, "Let's just put another hospital

bed in the living room, and it will be like dorm living." We did just that.

The afternoon Bruce came home, he had a bathroom emergency, so Kathleen called me, knowing the VNA would not come until the next morning. I went over. With a bedpan in my hand, I said to Bruce, "Let's pretend we do this every day!"

We got through it, and thus began my career. Thank you, Bruce and Kathleen, and Ann, and all the others.

After Kathleen and Bruce adjusted to their new arrangements, Kathleen called me and said they had two problems. First, they could not get the garbage to the curb, and second, they couldn't get the laundry done.

I said, "Praise God. You don't have any problems, because I am going to do those things for you."

Kathleen and Bruce spent eight more years in their home. Years later, when Kathleen died, her daughter sent me the teapot.

—❦—

Caring for Caring Suggestion: As you work with elders, view problems as a challenge to find the best possible solution, not simply the one that's easiest to implement.

2. The Power of Music

As long as we live, there is never enough singing.
—*Martin Luther*

One day I went in to help an elderly woman who had just been moved from her home in town to a darling cottage decorated to perfection by her three grown children. Sarah had dementia, and to her, this place did not look like her home. She scolded her children and was angry—very angry—for months. When the situation did not change, Sarah became depressed and stopped communicating with anyone.

When we met Sarah, we were not able to draw her out. We never heard her speak. But one day, one of our workers was flipping through the channels on Sarah's television and a rerun of *The Lawrence Welk Show* came on. Sarah perked right up and sang along with every word.

While previously we had been communicating with Sarah only through loving-kindness, at least now we knew how to give her pleasure and a sense of self—an ingredient that had been lacking in her life. And the truth is that this provided pleasure for us also. We began to include the fun task of searching for familiar music for all our clients. The response was overwhelmingly positive, even for those who did not have dementia.

———◦◦◦———

Caring for Caring Suggestion: Discover and honor your elders' interests to help them reconnect with their best sense of self.

3. The Power of Stories

After nourishment, shelter, and
companionship, stories are the thing
we need most in the world.

—*Philip Pullman*

As I recall my time with Prudence, I think of God's voice coming to the Magi in a dream to advise them to "go another way."

Prudence was crestfallen when she was confined to her hospital bed in the living room of her home. It was Christmas day, and she could no longer get out of bed to perform the duties of the mother to her seven grown children. She became more and more distraught—and very anxious—as her family gathered in the dining room without her.

I knew in advance that the day would be difficult for Prudence, so I brought a copy of a favorite book of mine to read to her.

I greeted Prudence by saying, "Hello! Jane here!" as I drew up a chair beside her bed. I told her that I had brought a wonderful story to read to her. However, Prudence was clearly feeling so undone that she could barely acknowledge my presence.

I said, "Please, may I read you this story?"

"No," she replied.

I let a few minutes pass in silence. Then I lowered the side railing and scooched in close. "You'll really like it!" I said. "It's *A Child's Christmas in Wales*, by Dylan Thomas."

"Oh, okay." She shrugged.

I read the story to Prudence. Her body language confirmed that she was engrossed. I read the final words a little while later: "I turned the gas down, I got into bed. I said some words to the close and holy darkness, and then I slept."

Just as I finished the story, I said, "That's it, Prudence."

"Is it over?" she said.

"Yes, it is."

Prudence raised her fists in the air and thrust them down sharply to demonstrate her disappointment that the book was over. Her gestures assured me that she had loved it and that it had made her Christmas more joyful.

It was joy for me too, as together we had found an unconventional way to celebrate Christmas. In fact, the memory has become so precious that I haven't felt the need to actually read the book since.

—◦◦◦—

Caring for Caring Suggestion: Visit elders with books in tow. Take time to talk about books in general to learn what the elder's favorites are. Share your thoughts about books.

4. The Power of Laughter

Mirth is God's medicine. Everybody ought to bathe in it.
—Henry Ward Beecher

I was hired by the son of Dorothy to set up a 24-7 arrangement for his mother. I explained that we worked as a team and that each of us would attempt to enrich Dorothy's life, as well as to attend to her needs.

I told the son that I always do the first shift myself so that I can become familiar with the client's needs and habits. This initial work enables me to pass on to my team suggestions on how we can be most helpful and affirming to the client and the family. The son took this opportunity to tell me that his mother was a rascal and would take any possible chance to play tricks on us.

The first shift with Dorothy was scheduled to last between 8:00 a.m. and 2:00 p.m. I met the son at Dorothy's house, and he said she was just about ready to get up out of bed for the day. He left, and I went up the stairs, calling softly, "It's Jane here, Dorothy. Time to get up."

Suddenly I heard a bloodcurdling scream from above me. My adrenaline shot off, and I barreled up the stairs. As I got closer, I could hear Dorothy cry, "I am dying! I am dying! I am dying!" When I arrived in her room, I found Dorothy curled into a fetal position.

I paused for a moment, observed the situation, and said, "Dorothy, this is my first shift—how would it look?"

Dorothy collapsed into laughter, knowing I had won the first round.

———

Caring for Caring Suggestion: Look for chances to join elders in their fun.

5. The Power of Poetry

Beauty is whatever gives joy.
—Edna St. Vincent Millay

Often people with dementia, regardless of the type, will repeat the same sentence over and over. Although this may initially seem pointless to the hearer, sometimes these words serve as avenues, opening up paths that allow us to go deeper into the senior's psyche.

Several years ago I worked with a client named Honey, who often said, "The butts of trees kept us warm. My father was a Maine lumberman."

One day, a question came to me: "What did your father do as a lumberman?" This ordinary question launched Honey into the wonderful revelation that she had adored her father and been very proud of him.

Honey told me that she had followed her father as a small child and watched in wonder as he surveyed a client's property and then accurately calculated in his head the price the owner could expect when the forest was properly timbered. Honey shared this information with great pride. Then she went on to say that while they walked the forest, her father had recited poetry from memory as he marked off the land and tagged the trees that were to be cut. In this way he created a legacy: a deeply embedded love of poetry, handed down tree by tree.

My delight continued as Honey recited some of the poems, which she had memorized a long time before.

> *I wandered lonely as a cloud*
> *That floats on high o'er vales and hills,*
> *When all at once I saw a crowd,*
> *A host of golden daffodils,*
> *Beside the lake, beneath the trees,*
> *Fluttering and dancing in the breeze …*

I discovered that I just had to give Honey the first line of a poem, and even though she was severely diminished by Alzheimer's, she could recite the rest of the poem.

What a source of enrichment for both of us! I was always grateful that I had found the path to help her move beyond that initial repetition of phrases.

———

Caring for Caring Suggestion: Watch for clues to identify what elders treasure most, and then tap into those hidden resources.

6. The Power of Simplicity

Yet all in order, sweet and lovely.

—*William Blake*

One of the most endearing things about my dear friend and client Charlotte—and trust me, there were a multitude of enduring, endearing things about Charlotte—was her love of simplicity.

Charlotte lived a Spartan life. Near the kitchen sink was an old clean tomato paste can. In it were a fork, a knife, a spoon, and a serrated knife. Charlotte used these tools every day and never complicated the issue by getting more out of the drawer.

Charlotte ate from one green bowl and one white plate. Today, a beloved worker, Kris Higgins, possesses the green bowl, and I have the white plate. Every time I take the plate down to eat, I smile as my mind automatically pictures Charlotte.

Charlotte's apartment surfaces were bare except for the coffee table, which held books and magazines that she deemed worthwhile. The television was masked by a piece of bright white ancient tatting with hospital corners folded in; this mask was removed only for the PBS news hour.

Nothing was complicated in Charlotte's life, and even though a series of ever-encroaching medical issues troubled her, we could always talk about what might be happening to her body. Her mind was never, praise God, an issue. Simplicity reigned.

There was a deep wisdom in Charlotte that we loved, and that wisdom was in knowing exactly what was necessary.

⸺◦◦◦⸻

Caring for Caring Suggestion: We each have our way, simple or complicated. Please honor the way of the particular elder with whom you are in touch.

7. A Promise between Friends

Promise only what you can deliver.
Then deliver more than you promise.

—*Author unknown*

A few years ago we started working with a new client—a ninety-two-year-old woman named Bertha. Bertha had been a schoolteacher. Actually, she never gave up that vocation. Her direct attitude, high expectations, and wonderful sense of humor still made her seem like a schoolmarm to us.

Every evening Bertha would speak with her friend Gladys Elwell Smith, who is also a dear friend of mine. At the end of the conversation, Bertha would always say, "I hope I wake up dead in the morning."

Gladys would answer, "You always say that."

Bertha would say it to us also: "I hope I wake up dead in the morning."

One day Bertha died, and we were all saddened.

Gladys had had a fall when she was ninety-three and ended up in the local nursing home, where I continued to visit her. Her rehabilitation treatment went well, and when I arrived one Wednesday I learned that she was scheduled to return home on that Friday.

That day we sat in bed together and laughed and carried on as usual. I told Gladys that I had gone through the book I was writing and had changed all the names to protect privacy.

"But your name—Gladys Elwell Smith—will not be changed," I promised her. "You will appear in my book."

Gladys said, "Oh no—you wouldn't! Oh, you rascal. Well, I *am* kind of flattered."

Gladys died that same night, and thus her full name appears in my book. I miss her terribly; this story is both a tribute to a wonderful woman and the keeping of my word to a friend.

—◦◦◦—

Caring for Caring Suggestion: When you have established a trust foundation with someone, be sure to follow through on your promises.

8. Transitions

In the night of death, hope sees a star,
and listening love can hear the rustle of a wing.
—Robert Ingersoll

I was called in to care for a woman who was transitioning from this world into the next. It is a sacred honor to assist an elder's passage through the veil as it grows thinner between this earthly place and the heavenly home reserved for each.

In this case, the veil was very thin, and we knew that she would die soon. As we waited, her ninety-two-year-old husband and their son, who was very gentle and tender toward both his parents, stayed at her side.

I kept June comfortable and clean and spoke gently with her of what was to come. I explained how I felt it was sacred work to be with her as she died. I engaged the son and husband in conversation around the bed so that I could better know them and be a better guide to June. They told me a story about a crow that June had adopted a few years before after witnessing the death of the crow's partner. The grieving crow would come twice a day and sit on the railing outside the dining room window and caw until June fed it.

Before June died, she blessed her son and husband by opening her eyes and smiling broadly at them. I see this kind of happening as flowers for the heart garden. Of course, the family members felt mixed emotions as the joyful experience and the time of death crossed over each other.

As I bathed June's body after her death, I told her each thing I was going to do as an act of honoring her. June was dressed as she had wished, and the three of us continued to sit with her as we waited for the undertaker to arrive.

I knew this might take some time, so after a while I suggested a cup of tea, which we drank sitting around the dining room table. Suddenly the crow appeared on the railing. This time, he did not caw, and I was sure he knew what had happened.

I suggested that perhaps the crow should have a whole slice of bread on such a day. The husband said nothing but got up and headed to the kitchen. As he reached the door, he turned to me and said, "I will give him a whole muffin, which he would prefer."

Ah, another flower for my heart garden.

———

Caring for Caring Suggestion: During transitions, keep your eyes, mind, and heart open. Flowers for the heart may appear at any time.

9. The Power of Organization

Be careful about reading health books.
You may die of a misprint.

—Mark Twain

As I began working for George, I realized that he was challenged by dementia—or, at the very least, a loss of short-term memory.

George had recently had cataract surgery, and the affected eye was causing problems. George had been sent home with a protocol of eye drops, which was difficult to follow, let alone implement.

I called the nurse at the doctor's office and explained that George could not follow the directions for his drops. The nurse said, "If the patient tells us he understands, we must accept that."

Yes, our national system of care is as difficult to follow as the directions George had been given. Our elders are continually teaching me how to understand society's ignorance.

George had six small white bottles of drops. Each bottle had the generic name on it. Each bottle was in a white box, which had the brand name on it. One drop needed to be applied to the eye seven times a day. The other drops were to be given either two, three, or four times a day.

I had to make a chart for myself simply in order to decipher the requirements. To help George, I then developed a chart and a corresponding color-coded system for the chart and the bottles of eye drops. I explained the chart to George a number of times, and in the end he was able to register and remember the specifics of his care.

The eye healed after a very long time. God is good.

———◦◦◦———

Caring for Caring Suggestion: Since medical instructions can be difficult to decipher, let alone follow, create charts and color-coded systems to help elders understand what to do. At the same time, always remember not to take any job away from the elders if they are able to do it correctly themselves.

10. The Power of Puppies

My little dog—a heartbeat at my feet.
—Edith Wharton

I first met Adam and Helen when their adult children, Carol and Micah, asked me to visit their parents. Helen's dementia was advancing, and their children's concerns for safety were heightening.

We had not announced my intentions yet at this point, because Adam and Helen were resistant to help of any kind. Instead, we simply had a nice chat in the living room as if I were just a visitor. After about half an hour, I excused myself, saying that I had a napping puppy in the car that might need airing.

Adam said, "I was wondering how you thought you were going to get out of here." There was laughter all around.

Then I countered, "Just for that, I am bringing the puppy in this house."

I did go to air the dog. Then I carried his tiny form in my two hands over to Helen and placed him in her lap. It was as if I had poured honey on her heart. She reacted to the puppy with uncontainable joy—and I brought him to visit her many times after that day.

—⟨⟨⟩⟩—

Caring for Caring Suggestion: Be alert for all possible enrichments for our elders, including the power of pets.

11. A Selfless Man

Life is an exciting business,
and most exciting when it is lived for others.

—Helen Keller

Steven was such a fine man. Goodness seemed to ooze from him like the natural flow of water over the stones in a brook: rippling, soothing, and giving out a constant renewal of self-esteem to us. He was always hiding the pain he was in, always feeling responsible for everyone's well-being.

Steven never sought comfort for himself. We did as he asked and allowed him to remain in control of his own being until the very end.

One evening I prepared his bed, gave him a bed bath, and helped him into clean pajamas. Then I pulled up the sides on his hospital bed.

"Good night," I said. "I wish I could reach in there and give you a hug."

He replied, "You just did."

I wish I could write a soaring tribute to his grace in the face of his agony and the knowledge of his oncoming separation from his family. I have never witnessed such love from a man for his children. I now know what a father's love should be.

What a gift to them—what a gift to me.

—⁙—

Caring for Caring Suggestion: Even when elders refuse specific types of help, you can still give them the gifts of respect, appreciation, and kindness—and enjoy the gifts they share too.

12. The Power of Gratitude

Gratitude is the memory of the heart.

—Jean Baptiste Massieu

Toward the end of her life, Doris experienced advanced degrees of Alzheimer's disease. However, with constant effort from her family and stimulation at every turn—including games, puzzles, cards, access to a piano, and a shuffle filled with her favorite music—she was unusual in that she frequently was able to stay present to us.

Throughout those days, Doris never lost her wonderful sense of humor or her ready smile. She was a joy for all of us to be with. She did, however, begin to drift away toward the end of her life, and on some days her presence shifted to a different decade.

Eventually, Doris suffered from a fall that began her descent into total confusion and disconnectedness. She was transferred between two hospitals before she was finally released and taken home. Hospice care arrived and set up a hospital bed in the living room so that she could look out at the ocean and also see the gas fire when it was lighted.

These moves equaled three changes of scenery, and Doris was confused by her surroundings. Even her own living room flummoxed her because of the hospital bed.

Akin to vaguely remembering a troubling dream, Doris

was aware of what she had suffered in the previous five days. Even though we had stayed 24-7 with Doris in the hospital, the damage was done. She had been assaulted by the constant traffic of unfamiliar faces and the ceaseless noise of the hospital loudspeaker announcements and buzzers. All these challenges are very disheartening to patients, particularly those who are elderly and suffer from dementia.

At that point, it seemed there was little we could do in terms of physical care to relieve her suffering. Doris had been sent home without a proper diagnosis, and though she still had pain in her ribs, the medication they had prescribed did not seem to relieve it.

Instead, we affirmed her value and her intelligence. We expressed that we knew it was hard to face changes in scenery and people.

The days passed with no improvement, and we all felt a great sadness as we neared the end of Doris's remarkable life. However, three days before her death, she suddenly experienced unbelievable clarity.

I was at my home, on the telephone with the worker who was at Doris's side. Doris must have been aware of our conversation, because she said, "If that is Jane, I need to speak with her."

When Doris took the line, I said, "Jane here, Doris, on this end of the phone."

Doris said, with utter clarity, "I want to thank you for

your mercy. It has been a rough couple of days, and your mercy enabled me to go to the funeral."

Astounding! Doris was referring to the time of her husband's funeral, a year and a half earlier. Now she was expressing appreciation for the moments I had cared for her as she had faced those very difficult days.

It was amazing to witness how the power of gratitude can break through barriers such as Alzheimer's. Doris's words were an affirmation for my heart. I had been completely unaware of Doris's recognition of mercy.

—⁓⁓—

Caring for Caring Suggestion: Don't be discouraged if your kindnesses appear to go unnoticed; gratitude is an emotion that fills the heart in mysterious ways.

13. The Power of Creation

Every artist dips his brush in his own soul,
And paints his own nature into his pictures.
—Henry Ward Beecher

Isabel was one of those unusual people who add so much to life and love that it is almost impossible to have enough adjectives to do her justice.

Isabel was in her mideighties when we met her. She was in the throes of dementia and had been diagnosed with Alzheimer's disease. The Alzheimer's left Isabel lacking short-term memory, but she was still able to remember many details of her earlier life. Isabel was also strong physically, as is often the case when a diagnosis of Alzheimer's is the correct one.

A gifted artist, Isabel would tell stories about her days of teaching art. She had always encouraged children to make big pictures—that is, to fill up the canvas.

Isabel was also a very gifted potter, though she had not created any pottery within recent years. As my coworker Sylvia and I looked around the wonderful kitchen and enjoyed the many bowls, lamps, dishes, and mugs that Isabel had created, Sylvia said, "Maybe once a potter, always a potter."

We spoke with a local pottery teacher and asked if we could bring Isabel to work at the wheel. We explained that we had no idea whether Isabel would even recall the act of making pottery, but we were looking to enrich her life, if possible. The teacher was very gracious and gave us a specific date to bring Isabel to the studio.

When we arrived with Isabel, we explained to her why we were there. At first, she was confused by some of the utensils, which she had likely never seen before. The potter explained their uses to Isabel to clear up any questions that might otherwise block her path.

The potter then sat Isabel down at a wheel and gave her a large portion of wet clay. Isabel placed the clay properly on the wheel, and as she started to work the clay and move the wheel, a transformation took place right before our eyes.

Isabel melded into the wheel. Suddenly she began to speak with the clay: "Bring your bubbles to the top." As she worked the clay into a bowl by spinning the wheel, she carried on a running conversation with the clay, encouraging it to cooperate and rise and allow itself to be shaped into some beautiful form. We were all astonished to see Isabel become the potter we had hoped for, and she enjoyed several more trips to the potter's wheel before she eventually moved away.

—∽∾∽—

Caring for Caring Suggestion: Look for ways to draw elders with Alzheimer's back into the present or the past, as the case may be.

14. The Power of Preparation

Expect the best, plan for the worst, and prepare to be surprised.
—Denis Waitley

A client of mine who was badly diminished by Alzheimer's disease and had virtually no short-term memory was suffering from pain in her knee. I took Simone to an orthopedic doctor for a shot to alleviate the pain.

I didn't want her to be surprised by the pain of the shot, so I considered my options. Because of my previous work with Alzheimer's patients, I knew Simone would need to have a warning—"It's going to hurt"—repeated over and over so that she heard it at the right time. Otherwise, she would likely forget the caveat by the time the pain arrived.

I told Simone she was going to have a shot in her knee to ease her pain and her walking difficulty. I told her the shot was going to hurt.

I kept repeating this while the doctor took his time preparing for the injection. After several rounds of listening to my warning, he glanced at me with disbelief.

Undeterred, I kept up my end of the job. "The shot is going to hurt; the shot is going to hurt; the shot is going to hurt. The shot—"

"Ouch, ouch."

I asked, "How was that injection?"

Simone said, "Didn't hurt."

—⟋∿⟍—

Caring for Caring Suggestion: Remember that goodness triumphs over ignorance.

15. The Power of Friendship

Friends are relatives you make for yourself.
—*Eustache Deschamps*

An old friend had hospice care arranged for himself when he asked me to come and set up care for him around the clock. He already had one worker who had been with him for years, but he wanted our assistance to supplement her help. Initially the case went along smoothly, and we were able to deliver our usual honoring, empowering care.

I always chose to do a shift on Sunday morning. I would bring my Bible, and just as the scriptures were being read at our church, I would read those scriptures to my friend. Then we would pray.

One day, out of the blue, my friend's daughter fired me. I was dismissed without even the courtesy of an explanation.

Shocked, hurt, and disheartened by this sudden turn of events, I struggled with how I could make it right with my friend. I decided I would call him. When he came on the line, I said, "John, we are going to spend all eternity together, so no hard feelings."

He replied, "God bless you."

—◦◦◦—

Caring for Caring Suggestion: When problems crop up with elders, take the high road. You will both benefit from it in the end.

16. Agreeing to Disagree

Hold a true friend with both your hands.

—*Nigerian proverb*

I first met Caroline at a meeting about eldercare in Rockport in the early 1990s. As a new person in town, I was forcing myself to attend meetings and become involved, but I was feeling less than confident.

During the meeting, attendees broke into smaller groups for discussion, and Caroline asked me if I could be the secretary of her smaller group. Despite my shyness, I agreed, although as we progressed in our discussion, it became apparent that as secretary I would be the one to give an oral report on our group to the entire assemblage. Oh my.

At the time, Caroline saw in me what I did not see in myself. She saw a capable person. I survived the talk, and Caroline and I went on to be friends. Oftentimes we would spend an evening together and discuss whatever topics intrigued us. We were not always on the same side of an issue, but we respected each other's opinions.

During the years of our friendship, she encouraged me to write stories. She was a poet and watercolorist. Now, as I sit with one of her harbor watercolors behind me, I am held up by Caroline's esteem.

One day, Caroline shared a dream with me. In the

dream, she was swimming in a circle of small islands. She swam to seven of the eight islands but not to the last one. Caroline asked what I thought it meant. I said only that the eighth island was out in front of her.

Years later, I was visiting one day as Caroline was in hospice care and failing. I suggested that perhaps it was time to swim to the eighth and final island. A few days later, Caroline left this earth. The eighth island remains a mystery.

⸺∾⸺

Caring for Caring Suggestion: Respect whatever happens in an elder's relationship with you.

17. Bunnies in Autumn

You can have the other words—chance,
luck, coincidence, serendipity.
I'll take grace. I don't know what it is exactly, but I'll take it.
　　　　　　　　　　　　　　　　—Mary Oliver

In the last few weeks before he died, Charles would ask our workers whether they had seen any bunnies outside. We were all saddened by this question, because while there were often bunnies in the yard in the summer months, it was November, so we would have to say, "No, Charles, not today."

Charles died at his home on November 29, with his wife, Eve, and most of his family by his side. After his last son arrived and had a chance to say good-bye, the family called the funeral home, and they came for Charles.

That night, Miriam, a friend, stayed on with Eve. At about one in the morning, Miriam went to the kitchen for water. She looked out the window, and there in the yard she saw several bunnies.

We told Eve this story over and over to compensate for her short-term memory loss. Eve loved to hear it again and again.

⌒ᗢᗢ⌒

Caring for Caring Suggestion: Even in times of death, keep open to the wonder and magic of life.

18. The Power of Choices

A peacefulness follows any decision, even the wrong one.
—Rita Mae Brown

The house was spare and calm and lovely. Sisters Christine and Gwen had been living together for some years, and Gwen had gradually become the caregiver for Christine, who was now dying.

I felt welcomed by the family's hospitality as soon as we were called in to help Gwen with her caregiving. During our initial meeting, their brother John was there to guide the discussion of what the family needed. John was nearly in tears as he expressed their gratitude for what we would bring in assistance and loving care.

Christine was still alert and very funny. Gwen played the role of overseer, but Christine didn't like it much and teased her without mercy.

One day, the hospice nurse told Gwen to ease off the food requirements because Christine should be allowed to eat whatever she wanted in her last days. The next morning when I went in, I found Gwen scandalized and Christine very jolly.

Gwen met me at the door with fist on hip. "Jane, do you want to know what Christine had for breakfast?"

"What?" I said, noting Gwen's horror.

"Bacon and a chocolate bar!"

Christine might not have had much time left, but she was determined to enjoy every minute.

———⟨◈⟩———

Caring for Caring Suggestion: At the end of life, avoid unnecessary restrictions with food. Ask for the green light from the doctor, and let the dying person have some fun.

19. Bunny's Closet

Few delights can equal the mere presence of one we trust utterly.
—George MacDonald

We took care of Nancy Smith for a number of years. She was fondly known as Bunny. Bunny had Alzheimer's. Her words were few. So when we asked questions, we watched her face for clues. Over time, we learned to communicate simply by sculpting our questions carefully.

Bunny lived in the home of her supportive daughter, Beth. We went in mostly at night to be sure Bunny was safe and that Beth was able to rest. We also went in on Sundays so Beth could attend services at her beloved church, Saint Mary's Episcopal in Rockport, Massachusetts.

When we went at night, Bunny was often in bed when we arrived. Most nights, however, she would get up a few hours later, empty her closet, and then put everything back. She would empty her closet and then put everything back. She would empty her closet and then put everything back. You get the picture. We helped.

Sometimes this went on for hours. We resembled the synchronized movement of the sandpipers at the edge of the waves. It was exhausting for us but not for Bunny. Bunny was being productive.

One night when I was there with Bunny, she actually

slept through the night. In the morning, I leaned over Bunny to wish her a good morning.

I said, "Oh, Bunny, I can tell by your expression that you have no idea who I am."

Bunny replied, "No, but I trust your face."

Trust was our reward for listening—and for treating her with love and respect as we helped her do what she wished to do with no complaints.

———⁂———

Caring for Caring Suggestion: Be sure trust is the foundation of any relationship.

20. The Power of Prayer

Greet one another with a holy kiss.

—Romans 16:16

We had been working with Jane and Elizabeth for only a week when Elizabeth took a downward turn. During my next visit I chanced to whisper to her, "Are you scared?"

"Yes, I am, a little," she replied.

I said, "Even though you have your faith, Elizabeth, you are about to do a new thing, and that is always scary. But," I continued, "you can always take the Bible's word of truth that you are loved by God, and He has prepared a place for you when you cross from this world to the next."

I asked if she would like to pray together. When she said yes, I took both of her hands in mine, and we pulled in close to each other. I followed her lead as we prayed for courage, the desire to leave this world behind, and the will to move on to the elsewhere prepared for her. Elizabeth closed our prayer time by thanking God for my presence with her. After we said our amens, we kissed, and for the first time I understood the words of Romans 16:16: "Greet one another with a holy kiss."

One day later, after we had known her for only one week, Elizabeth died, and I cried for the loss of such a wonderfully spirited person. If any light shines from me, it is a reflection of the elders I have been privileged to know.

⚘

Caring for Caring Suggestion: If the elders would like to pray, let them take the lead.

21. The Power of Patience

Patience is also a form of action.

—*Auguste Rodin*

Sometimes we would stay with Harriette overnight. One night I remained awake upstairs while Harriette slept downstairs.

I was enjoying the summer night air coming in through the open windows, wafting the light curtains into the room so it looked like a Wyeth painting.

Suddenly my reveries turned to a nose-crinkling horror as the smell of skunk spray burst into the house.

I heard Harriette stirring below as the smell reached her nostrils. By the time I got downstairs, she was wide awake, alarmed because she thought the smell was coming from the gas stove.

I explained that a skunk had sprayed in the garden, which caused momentary relief for Harriette. However, her loss of short-term memory function meant that her mind erased this information almost immediately, and she quickly reverted to the fear of gas. We spent the rest of the night sitting up downstairs.

Harriette: "Is that gas I smell?"

Me: "No, a skunk sprayed in the garden."

Harriette: "Oh, good …"

Harriette: "Is that gas I smell?"

Me: "No, a skunk sprayed in the garden."

Harriette: "Oh, good ..."

Harriette was truly frightened by the smell, and anything less than a soft repetition of the truth would have been less than fair.

—◦∞◦—

Caring for Caring Suggestion: Always practice patience, a God-given gift that is often necessary when working around, amid, and between short-term memory losses.

22. The Power of Acceptance

Once we accept our limits, we go beyond them.

—*Albert Einstein*

During the past few years, I've been intrigued by a couple of articles that have appeared in the *New York Times* regarding how people with dementia can benefit from going to museums and being exposed to great works of art.[2] Though Susan James, one of our clients, did not have dementia, her physical diminishments had stalled her work as a watercolor artist. At ninety-two, her legs were not strong, and she was very hard of hearing.

Speaking through a device for expanding sound, I asked Susan whether she would like to go see the Monet exhibit at the Museum of Fine Arts. She felt there would be too much walking, but I assured her that they had wheelchairs available in the lobby of the museum.

She initially refused, stating that she had never used a wheelchair before and was not about to start doing so now. She said she'd feel humiliated in a wheelchair, which would announce that her body was weakened.

I leaned into the speaker and said, "Wheelchair/ Monet. No wheelchair/no Monet."

---

2   See Randy Kennedy, "The Pablo Picasso Alzheimer's Therapy," *The New York Times,* October 30, 2005, and Karen Jones's "Keeping Those With Alzheimer's Engaged," *The New York Times,* March 12, 2009.

After careful consideration, Susan chose Monet. At the museum, we used a wheelchair to view each painting slowly. The best part for me was the commentary that Susan provided the whole way through. Susan shared her knowledge and opinions on each painting.

We talked about it for weeks. We reviewed what we had seen through a book we had purchased in the museum shop.

This was possible only because Susan had finally accepted both her own limitations and the benefits of a wheelchair. From that day forward, we used one often for other engaging road trips. Eventually we got her one of her own.

———

Caring for Caring Suggestions: Help elders accept their limits so that you can break some of their barriers together.

23. The Power of Seeds

She spied lupines that grew from seed blown from her garden. And then she knew what she could do to bring beauty to the world ...
—Barbara Cooney, Miss Rumphius

One of our dear clients, Mary, was about to leave our area to move nearer her daughter in upstate New York. I was scheduled for a visit that morning to say good-bye. Mary, though confused by Alzheimer's disease, was capable of occasionally being in the moment with us.

I had not slept well, as I was awfully sad that Mary was moving. I loved and admired her very much. I struggled to figure out what I could say to her that would allow her to remember our experiences together.

Finally I decided I would take a copy of *Miss Rumphius*, a children's book written and illustrated by Barbara Cooney. It is a story about a little girl who is told by her grandfather that she can do what she wants with her life, but she must do something that will make the world more beautiful.

I impressed upon Mary that she had spent her entire life spreading seeds of creativity, charm, love, and joy— just as Miss Rumphius had spread far and wide her lupine seeds to make the world more beautiful. We went over and over the story and the connection between Mary and Miss Rumphius.

I gave Mary my copy of *Miss Rumphius* to take with her to remind her how wonderful she was—words repeated many times by her daughter during the years they enjoyed living near each other.

———— ✿✿✿ ————

Caring for Caring Suggestion: Show appreciation by reminding elders of the valuable seeds they have spread throughout their lives to make the world a better place.

24. A Happy Ending

Only in the darkness can you see the stars.
—Martin Luther King Jr.

One day a client, Patty, went out for her daily walk. Patty was well advanced in the journey of Alzheimer's, but up to this point her husband, Timothy, had felt that she was still clearheaded enough to take a routine walk by herself. It was her custom to walk up Landmark Lane, down Drumlin past Parker Pit (a small quarry), and then come around Granite Street to return home.

It would have been cruel, to my way to thinking, to deny this freedom to Patty. We have the blessing to live in a small town, so everyone knew Patty. There was little traffic, and Patty had the trip down pat. I had observed that most Alzheimer's patients did certain routines robotically, *but* that did not diminish their joy at being free.

At any rate, off she went on this particular day, which at first seemed like any other. However, this day was different, because she did not come home at the expected time.

I went out in my car and drove around but could not find her. I drove back to the house and suggested that we should call the police. Timothy was adamant that we avoid this step as long as possible, because seeing the police might alarm her, so I agreed to check one more time.

I went out again in the car and warily checked the quarry as I drove slowly around. No Patty. I went back to the house to insist that we needed to call the police. Just then, the phone rang. It was the police, saying that a man had called to say he had a stranger in his house. The address he gave was just five houses away from Patty's house.

The man who found her, a fisherman, had gone out very early, as fishermen do, and he had left his house a mess. When he'd returned around five o'clock in the evening and stepped into his home, he had very quickly become aware that something was different. It was cleaned and picked up, with dishes done, bed made, and everything neat. He walked into the living room, and there was Patty, sitting and waiting for Timothy. The man spoke kindly to her and left the room to call the police, who then called Timothy.

When I picked Patty up, the man was so kind. He hugged Patty good-bye and said she could come again. Patty was pleased to see me and also pleased that she had helped someone. This was a happy conclusion to a very distressing afternoon.

When I related this story to my friend Jill Burke, she said, "Could you drop Patty off in my neighborhood?"

—◦◦◦—

Caring for Caring Suggestion: Seek freedom for your elder whenever safely possible.

25. The Power of Memory

We do not remember days; we remember moments.
—Cesare Pavese, The Burning Brand

I have learned from my time working with elders that when people have been truly shocked by an event, they will often remember it despite dementia or other problems with memory.

After his stroke, Earl was considerably diminished physically, but after setting him up downstairs, we honored his request to help him with one more trip upstairs to collect his favorite things. We told him to call us when he was finished so we could help him come back down.

Instead, after selecting the items he wanted, Earl decided to make the trip back downstairs on his own. When I suddenly noticed that Earl was at the top and about to start down to the first step, I headed up and told him to wait for me.

He said, "I'm okay!"—as he began to tumble down the stairs. I quickly retreated down since I knew I could not stop his fall and we would both be injured if he hit me. Then his wife, Lauren, and I watched, horrified, as he banged on each step.

When Earl landed at the bottom, he never lost consciousness. He looked at us and said, "I think we're okay—I landed on my head."

Not only do these words reflect his sense of humor, but the story is also important because, despite her challenges with memory, Lauren never forgot that incident and spoke of it often.

A year or so later, when Earl was dying in the hospital bed that now had been added to the dining room, I asked a friend to tell Lauren what was happening so that she would be fully aware. The friend indicated that it would do no good because Lauren would forget it anyway.

However, when Lauren and Earl and I were alone, I grabbed Lauren's arms, shook her gently, and said, "Lauren, Lauren, I need to know you understand that Earl is dying, and if you have anything to say, you must say it now."

Lauren replied, "Can I get in bed with him?"

I replied, "Of course. I will help you."

I got Lauren in and put pillows behind her so that the railing would not hurt her. Lauren stayed in bed with Earl for hours and talked softly nonstop.

Lauren never lost track of the fact that Earl was dying.

—————

Caring for Caring Suggestion: Assume that elders with dementia can process issues at some level, and try to honor their right to know.

26. A Strong Sense of Humor

Every survival kit should include a sense of humor.
—*Author unknown*

Through word of mouth, our team was recommended to care for a woman who was returning home after multiple trips to the hospital with the threat of heart attack. The family had secured the services of hospice and asked us to give them 24-7 care in addition to that. Though I knew I didn't have enough workers to give them that many hours, I felt called to be with them, so I agreed to do it, planning to fill in the overtime myself.

When I first met the woman, she told me with a glint in her eye that she had always thought having a heart attack was easy, but she had been back and forth four times to the hospital trying to have her heart attack. She was facing reality head on and having fun.

One of my most faithful workers, Kelly, agreed to go the first afternoon and stay overnight. Kelly reported that they had spent a restless night together.

When it was my turn to stay overnight, we also got off to a very restless start. However, during the course of the night we were able to juggle the meds with permission from hospice. Finally she was peaceful, and she was able to fall asleep toward morning.

When she awakened, she said, "I am surprised we

are all still here this morning!" What a woman—fun the whole way.

The next day was Saturday, and many of her family came to visit. When I returned that evening, my client was very happy and told me she loved having her family there. We took turns keeping her company.

A few hours later, she began to feel poorly and asked to use the commode. I helped her to the commode, and she had a heart attack while I was holding her. I called for oxygen, and I called for the family. They came quickly and helped me get her back into bed. We made her comfortable. As best I could, I told the family what I believed was happening as we sat with her. Suddenly her breathing changed, and she died.

It was a privilege to be with this fabulous woman at such a sacred time and to be with her extremely sensitive family. We workers each ache with the want to have the sharing continue, but we know we must move on.

—◦◦◦—

Caring for Caring Suggestion: Encourage humor in any circumstance.

27. A Light in the Darkness

God gave us memory so that we might have roses in December.
—James M. Barrie

It was already truly dark outside at 4:15 p.m. a few days after Christmas. Brigit, who suffered from Alzheimer's and short-term memory loss, did not like the dark. However, I knew from speaking with the family that Brigit had not been out to see the Rockport, Massachusetts, town Christmas tree that year.

I asked Brigit if she would go out with me in the car to see the tree. She looked out the window at the darkness and declined to go. I teased. I cajoled. I offered to warm up the car for her. She finally said yes, and off we went in a toasty car, proving I am a woman of my word.

I wanted to surprise Brigit with the beauty of the Christmas tree. With that in mind, I drove up High Street and then down Broadway to the little lighthouse in the middle of the intersection. I told Brigit to get ready to see a beautiful sight. Then I swung the car into Dock Square to reveal the Christmas tree.

Brigit raised her hands in the air and said, "Has it ever been more wonderful!" We drove slowly past the tree so Brigit could really take in the spectacle of our Rockport town tree.

I drove around Dock Square, down School Street,

and then down Broadway to the lighthouse again; an idea was stirring in my brain.

I swung the car into Dock Square again, after telling Brigit to get ready to see a beautiful sight. Brigit raised her hands in the air and said, "Has it ever been more wonderful!"

With that idea tickling my brain, we did this routine seven times, with Brigit having the same reaction each time I swung the car toward the tree.

Finally we went home, both of us tired but happy after our trip.

The next day the tree fell in the wind, and the Department of Public Works cut it up and hauled it away. I raced to tell Brigit the news.

Despite her dementia and memory challenges, her immediate response was, "It's a good thing we did it good yesterday."

A Christmas miracle had happened. I took this story and applied the same repetition technique to all my dementia patients, often with similar levels of success. What wisdom Brigit had given us! What a gift!

—◈—

Caring for Caring Suggestion: Consider repeating enjoyable experiences to help elders remember them.

28. A Small Loaf of Bread

We can't help everyone, but everyone can help someone.
—*Ronald Reagan*

Ethel, age ninety-two, was a friend of my beloved client Gertrude, who was also age ninety-two. Ethel was a tiny, vigorous woman who held an all-encompassing world view and filled in Gertrude, who was hard of hearing, on all the international news and, of course, the local tidbits.

Ethel always brought Gertrude a small loaf of bread that she had baked herself that morning. I served tea and toast as they chatted in the living room.

One day I overheard Ethel saying that she had difficulty getting her laundry done since she lived on the second floor in her downtown apartment in Rockport. I confessed to overhearing and offered to do her laundry for her. Ethel, always gracious, accepted help to counterbalance all that she gave out.

I didn't have a washer and dryer either, but I was more able to manage the stairs, and this task gave me a better chance to visit Ethel regularly. Ethel was an elder who lived alone. When I delivered Ethel's laundry, I received a small loaf of bread in exchange. The dual benefits are obvious.

One day as I was driving by Ethel's building, it popped into my head to stop in and say hello, even though there wasn't any laundry/bread exchange set up. I rang the bell downstairs and trudged up the winding stairs. As I approached the door, Ethel opened it and fell into my arms. I moved her to the couch and dashed for the telephone to call 911.

It turned out that Ethel had had a heart attack, and I felt like a knight on a shiny steed.

Ethel survived, thankfully, with only minor aftereffects, and the laundry/bread brigade went forward successfully for several more years.

⎯◦◦◦⎯

Caring for Caring Suggestion: Trust your instincts; an elder may need your help.

29. The Power of Laughter

Laughter is the shortest distance between two people.
—*Victor Borge*

Sometimes our time with an elder is just plain fun.

We helped June with her shower, but that was the only personal care she required. We were companions, and we had very good times.

One day we went out in the car to see the ocean and get an ice cream. When we returned, I pulled into June's driveway, got out on my side, and went around to June's side of the car. I opened the passenger door for her and started to walk toward the house. June did not want any assistance—ever.

As I walked forward, I saw a big piece of paper in the driveway. I bent over from my waist to pick it up, and the seat of my pants split horizontally. We laughed and laughed together.

When we were finished laughing, June said, "You did that just so I would have a laugh."

It would have been worth it if I had.

Caring for Caring Suggestion: Share laughter with elders whenever you can.

30. The Third Pair of Boots

A good time to laugh is any time you can.
—Linda Ellerbee

I remember working with a wonderful client named Teresa. Initially our time together involved just companionship. We walked and talked and enjoyed sharing spiritual outlooks.

We had eggs together. Whenever I poached eggs for us, Teresa wanted some egg water put on her toast. I always obliged but refrained from having water on my own toast. Still, I put this bit of knowledge in the back of my head so that I would always prepare the eggs and toast the way she liked them. It doesn't take much of an effort to make a senior feel special.

One day, Teresa started talking about the coat closet by the front door.

"What would you like to happen in there, Teresa?" I asked.

"I really want to clean it out, but I hate to let anything go."

"Ah, my dear, you have met your match."

So we started on the closet, and we put a few things aside to go to charity. However, when I suggested that the third pair of boots should go, Theresa objected, and thus ensued a tug-of-war to beat all tugs-of-war.

We began to laugh as we tugged the boots back and forth between us. It was a kids' game. I tugged. Teresa tugged. At the end we collapsed into laughter, and for the rest of our time together, our game of tug-of-war became a secret laugh between us.

———⟊⟊⟊———

Caring for Caring Suggestion: Don't forget to lighten up!

31. Church Flowers

In union there is strength.

—*Aesop*

When my elders express their needs, I always listen attentively and validate what they are experiencing and where they happen to be in their minds. Their desires may sometimes seem to be gibberish or out of chronological order or just plain nonsensical. However, this is not so; instead, they simply reflect what the elders are experiencing at certain moments as they move toward the end of their lives and feel compelled to tie up loose ends.

For example, Prudence, who was resting in her hospital bed in the dining room, became very anxious one day. She began to rapidly knead the edge of the sheet with her fingers, and she became terribly restless.

I sat with Prudence, and after a while I said, "Prudence, what is the trouble? You seem so disquieted."

She said strongly, "I want those flowers there to go to the church."

"Where is the church?" I asked.

"Over there," she said, pointing toward the living room.

"I can do that for you, Prudence," I said. I took the

flowers into the living room and set them down where Prudence could see them.

Peace reigned the rest of the evening.

Caring for Caring Suggestion: Validate the elder's experience to prevent further agitation and to give the elder a sense of connection to reality. If an elder's experience is not being validated as it occurs, the emotional needs escalate when they could so easily be calmed.

32. In through the Back Door

Happiness often sneaks in through a door
you didn't know you left open.

—*John Barrymore*

My team at Caring for Caring had the great privilege to work with Henry and Betty for many years, but it certainly took us some effort to get there.

Henry and Betty had a blended family that included four sons on one side and three daughters on the other side. All the children were very devoted to their parents.

When the grown children first asked us to become involved as caregivers, I went to visit Henry and Betty, as is my custom, to get acquainted and try to convince these two elders that they needed some help to stay home and be as free as they had been all their married life. In the convincing department I failed. They assured me that they absolutely did not need assistance of any kind.

I reported my failure to one of the daughters, who was the vital family contact for me. I assured her that I would continue to visit and try to make a roadway into their lives.

This is a most difficult part of my job as the founder of a tiny agency for in-home care. People generally resist help of any kind. I continued to visit and quickly learned that Betty and Henry were brilliant and wise and generous in spirit. They always took the high road no matter the circumstances. However, despite my continued attempts, I was unable to make any inroads.

Finally, at one point Henry had a pacemaker implanted, so the VNA nurses came in to see that all was well. This service to our elders is often provided after a hospital stay or when someone is coming out of rehabilitation and going home.

On one particular day, I dropped by as the nurse was discharging Henry from her service. The couple asked me why I was there after the nurse had left.

Being an opportunist, I said that I represented the next group of people who follow the VNA nurses. A stretch by any measure, but it got me in the door. And so began a long and loving relationship between this couple and Caring for Caring, which ultimately proved to be a wonderful experience for all.

—◦◦◦—

Caring for Caring Suggestion: Practice perseverance to ensure that elders get the care they need.

33. Over Yonder

The warbler
Amid the bamboo shoots
Sings of old age

—*Basho*

Helen became a client after a number of years of friendship. We took long walks together every morning. One of the things I cherish about Helen many years later is her expression "over yonder," which she would use when she was pointing something out to me on our walks.

Today I use this expression as often as I can, because the memories of our walks together bring joy to my heart.

―⁓―

Caring for Caring Suggestion: Enjoy the present moment, and see the world through the elder's eyes.

34. Always There

The world is not outside you.

—Ramana Maharshi

Some elders may struggle to conjure up specific words, but their basic selves are always there, waiting to speak up, no matter how old or how diminished they may be. Here's an example.

Elaine was disenchanted (to put it mildly) with the nursing home where her husband was a patient. Peter had rheumatoid arthritis and Alzheimer's disease. He could not use his hands, which meant he needed to be fed, but the way the staff backhanded his food on a spoon was very demeaning. The Alzheimer's also seemed to us to render Peter invisible to the nursing home staff, even though with prepping he was able to respond to us with smiles and nods. These were just two of Elaine's issues with the institution. I told Elaine I would not leave her side if she wanted to bring Peter home from the nursing facility.

By the time Elaine had successfully arranged to bring Peter home, he was more or less uncommunicative. When the EMTs carried and rolled Peter's gurney to the kitchen door, they discovered that it was too wide for the entrance. As they backed up to head for the front door, Peter yelled, "Don't take me back!"

We quickly explained the situation to Peter, settled him into his hospital bed in the master bedroom, and made him comfortable with constant words of reassurance. Peter said nothing further.

A few days later, in preparation for the nurse's arrival, I was doing gentle exercises with Peter, explaining each movement as I flexed his extremities and massaged his back and shoulders. I told him that I was limbering him up so that when the nurse came and rolled him over to give him a shot, he would be less stiff and the roll would be less painful.

Peter raised his head off the pillow slightly, and said, "I appreciate your foresight, your hindsight, and your insight."

I was astounded and overjoyed with this statement. It was so "Peter like" that it assured me that he was still available to us and enjoying our ministrations.

I replied, "My pleasure, Peter."

I dashed out of the room to tell Elaine what he had just said. Not only was Elaine delighted, but at a deeper level, she had received affirmation that bringing Peter back to his seaside home was the right thing to do.

It turned out that those were Peter's last words—a gift from him to assure us he was responding and loving our gentle care, even when that fact was not readily apparent to us.

—⁓—

Caring for Caring Suggestion: Take heart in knowing that the elders appreciate your care even when there are no obvious signals.

35. In the Kitchen

As one egg is like another.

—Cervantes

Isabel had advanced Alzheimer's disease—and *dis-ease* it was. Although she was calm, creative, and a lovely, warm person during the day, each afternoon around four o'clock Isabel would have a change in personality that made her very jealous and demanding. This behavior, which is known as "sundowning," is not uncommon for people with Alzheimer's.

During the dinner preparations, she insisted that no one but George, her husband, could be in the kitchen. She had always prepared his meals and certainly was not going to stand interference. The Caring for Caring worker would sit in the hall with the idea of surreptitiously altering anything that was dangerous or poisonous. George had some very odd combinations of food, but he ate it with patience.

As noted, this behavior occurred only at the end of the day. In contrast, when it was time for breakfast, Isabel would be her usual wonderful self, and even though she suffered from a lack of short-term memory, each morning she would ask George what kind of egg he would like to have. George always answered, "Could you fry me an egg?"

"Of course," Isabel would answer and proceed—every day—to scramble him an egg.

I would exchange eyebrow-raising with him, with our smiles behind our hands.

—◦◦◦—

Caring for Caring Suggestion: Smile with elders about the small issues to help them navigate the big ones.

36. The Best Approach

Be beautiful if you can, wise if you want to,
but be respected—that is essential.

—Anna Gould

Each client has special and separate needs, but I pay close attention to details and do everything possible to affirm and empower each senior. Our words and actions must never detract from an elder's self-esteem.

When Ethel was confined to a hospital bed, she often needed help with her drinks. Each time I took a drink with a straw to her, I made eye contact and created an excuse as to why I would hold the glass for her as she reached for the drink.

"I've filled the glass too full, Ethel; may I hold it for you?"

Similarly, sometimes when my coworker Kelly would finally manage to get an Alzheimer's patient into the shower, the client would be lost as to what to do next. Kelly would say, "Could I wash your hair? I just love the smell of your shampoo."

Phrases like these skirt the real issue and do not offend, making it so easy to be the most thoughtful.

Caring for Caring Suggestion: Each thing we do for elders can boost their self-esteem or tear it down, so choose your words and actions carefully.

37. Calling the Shots

It's not hard to make decisions when you
know what your values are.

—Roy Disney

When we first called on Constance, she was sitting at her very modern laptop, writing a book. She was ninety-two years old and failing as far as her physical health was concerned. Otherwise, she was sharp as a tack. Her daughter simply wanted us to help out in any way that Constance desired.

Constance worked daily on her book. She held strongly to her faith as a Swedenborgian and instructed each of us about her religion. Through Constance, we acquired a profound sense that life was precious and should be shared without hesitation.

Her arena was getting smaller (as is the case with most elders). Typically, the space our elders occupy narrows down to two rooms and then to one room. Next, the bathroom is given up for a commode. Eventually each elder ends up in a bed, and that becomes the last place of residence on this earth.

For Constance the kitchen was her next-to-last stand. Constance ate mostly soups and smoothies. For breakfast, she'd ask us to make her one vegetable smoothie and one fruit smoothie. We noticed (how could we not?)

that some of the fruits and vegetables were a little old. However, Constance insisted that she must use them up, no matter what. She watched us like a hawk lest we throw away something she considered still good.

We did make the smoothies exactly as she wanted. I explained to the Caring for Caring workers that Constance was down to her bedroom and her kitchen, so we must let her reign in the kitchen. I instructed them to put down the knife and pick up the scissors if that was what Constance wished them to do. This was her world now, and she needed to be in charge in every way, to the letter. Constance, aware of our intentions, freely bossed us around.

In addition to honoring Constance's wishes in the kitchen, we initially worked with the fact that Constance did not like being touched. However, as she neared her death, she finally agreed to a foot rub and then took on a full body massage. It turned out that she loved it, and we teased her about taking so long to learn the pleasure of a rubdown. We laughed together about it, and I kept rubbing.

In the end, Constance waited for her last grandson to come, and then she died—maintaining a sense of respect and control until her very last breath.

———

Caring for Caring Suggestion: Let elders call the shots as much as possible to help them retain a sense of control.

38. A Close-Knit Life

Great peace is found in little busy-ness
—Geoffrey Chaucer

When we first went in to work for Ellen, she was newly back from rehabilitation after a replaced hip.

Initially Ellen would not respond to any of my questions. I thought perhaps it was the transition from a facility to home that had made Ellen reticent. It turned out that I was asking questions about food, and Ellen really only liked two things: poached eggs on white toast and cream cheese and olives on white bread. No vegetables. No salads. *No* tomatoes. I guess she thought I would give her a hard time. However, I figured if she had lived this long on such a diet, she could go on with that diet. I gave her what she wanted, and once she realized this would happen, we became fast friends.

We enjoyed helping Ellen, who had a large and loving family. She was a hoot. But perhaps the most memorable thing about her was her devotion to her hobby, which helped her relax and kept her productive. She knitted: *click, click, click* went the needles.

A year after we started working with her, Ellen went out to play bridge one afternoon. She came home late on that day. She turned on the TV and began to knit. Ellen died sitting right there—content and productive to the very end. We were happy and sad at the same time. It was a loss for us, but she had not suffered.

———✦———

Caring for Caring Suggestion: Encourage elders to pursue hobbies and remain as active and productive as they can.

39. The Blessings of a June Fall

Friendship isn't a big thing—it's a million little things.
—Author unknown

Really, Charlotte and I were chosen sisters. We met at a town event and bonded strongly.

Over the years, we shared many things, but mostly Charlotte shared her wisdom of ninety-two years with me. We shared books and the discussion of them. We shared spirituality and the discussion of it.

Charlotte taught me many things that I felt I should have already known—given my fifty-five years—such as the meaning of a "June fall."

One June day, after Charlotte had become a client so we could help her stay in her home, we were out for our usual daily walk. Down the steep street from Charlotte's house there was an apple tree. Charlotte told me that every apple tree had a June fall. The tree pushed off the apples that were weakest to make assurances for future trees and to ensure a good harvest. We agreed that this tree, though untended by any humans, would have a good harvest in the fall.

I arrived at Charlotte's house one afternoon in late September to be greeted by the smell of apples cooking.

"Where did you get the apples?" I asked.

The answer did not surprise me. "From our June-fall

tree down the hill. I carried two canes with me and leaned on one and banged the branches of our tree with the other."

"You are so dangerous, Charlotte!"

"Have some applesauce, Jane?"

It was the best applesauce I've ever had—warm and sweet and prepared by my sister, who was a very determined person.

—⁓—

Caring for Caring Suggestion: Remain open to the wisdom of the elders; you never know what you may learn!

40. The Language of Friendship

The language of friendship is not words but meanings.
—Henry David Thoreau

One of my first jobs was with Vera, a very shy elderly woman who was confined to her bed. I always announced myself when going up the stairs to her room. "It's me, Vera—Jane, coming up the stairs. Not an elephant, as you might think."

I read to Vera and once in a blue moon had a little chat, but mostly Vera remained behind a veil of shyness.

Vera was horrified to be exposed, so whenever possible I changed her with the blanket as a tent over my head. Though she did not say anything, I knew in my heart that she was grateful for my respect of her shyness.

Sometimes I would cook apples on the stove downstairs so the smell would waft up the stairs and bring its pleasure to Vera.

Vera was a gentle soul, and I loved her and thought of her as a bowl of pink light shining in her corner of the world.

Caring for Caring Suggestion: Appreciate elders exactly as they are, and morph yourself into what they need.

41. Through the Walls of Memory

My patients taught me not how to die, but how to live.
—Elisabeth Kübler-Ross

One day after her ninety-fourth birthday, when the appraisers came to look at Honey's house, her family decided not to tell her who they were or why they were there. However, I knew that Honey was running out of money and the house was to be put on the market.

Apparently Honey had had a sixth sense about it, and she had a heart attack that day. We called in hospice and kept her at home. The sale of the house would have to wait.

She was set up in a bed by a window downstairs, and I set up a perch for birdseed just outside that window. Oftentimes when Honey rolled over to do her ritual of snapping up the shade to start the day, she'd find a very brazen squirrel on the perch having breakfast. Honey was always horrified that he was eating the birds' food, and she would rap on the windowpane until the squirrel scurried away.

As Honey began a slow descent physically, we met her every need and kept her spirits up. She never lost her sense of humor, often tossing stuffed animals at us and laughing at our surprise.

One evening I was to sleep over with Honey. Suddenly I realized from her breathing pattern that she was close to death.

I leapt over everything in my path and grabbed the Bible on my way to her bedside. I pulled up a chair and held her hand and read the Twenty-third Psalm. At once I realized that with her short-term memory loss, she would forget I had read her the Twenty-third Psalm as soon as I stopped. I decided to read it over and over, until one precious tear ran down Honey's lovely, pale cheek into the hem of her sheet.

Soundlessly Honey transitioned from this world to the next. The only noise in the house was the sound of my own sorrow as Honey left.

—◦◦◦—

Caring for Caring Suggestion: Follow your heart's wisdom whenever conventional actions won't work.

42. The Power of Fun

Never, ever underestimate the importance of having fun.
—Randy Pausch

Sometimes the clients with dementia surprise us with what they *can* remember. Each evening, I would help Beatrice, who suffered from short-term memory loss, to set up the coffeepot. We would pretend the coffee fairy came in the night and made our coffee for us.

Utter joy filled me as I served Beatrice coffee in bed the next morning, and she said, "Ah, the coffee fairy did come."

How wonderful that her penchant for fun was able to triumph over her struggles to remember the recent past.

———

Caring for Caring Suggestion: Make fun a top priority in your relationships with elders.

43. "Carry On"

*Death is simply a shedding of the physical body, like
the butterfly coming out of a cocoon … It's like putting
away your winter coat when spring comes.*
—Elisabeth Kübler-Ross

My friend Sarah Wetzel came to me one afternoon and told me that her friend Margot, a very intelligent woman and a masterful singer and treasury of music, was dying. Margot wanted to stay home to die, but she did not have the money to hire any help.

I immediately discussed the situation with my coworker, Ann, who agreed that we should both take on this special case for a much-reduced fee. I did not want anyone to feel beholden, so we charged five dollars a visit. Then I told Sarah, "Take me to your friend."

We went to Margot's humble home. I sat with her on the couch, and we talked about what Caring for Caring could provide for her. She was humble and able to accept this special arrangement graciously.

During her final days, Margot was barely able to speak, but Ann and I communicated and met her needs. Margot's courage in the face of death enriched us more than words could ever have done.

Margot received hospice care, and we worked well as a team. During her last few weeks, a dozen of her incredible friends took turns sleeping over so that Margot would not be alone. One morning I sent out word to these women that soon their friend would die. They came and gathered at the bedside. Because of the love of these women, Margot was read to and sung to and blessed with many blessings.

With the words "Carry on," Margot died that day and left us all stunned by our loss.

Together we bathed Margot, as is our custom after death. The friends were so respectful of Margot, and it seemed that they loved her with one heart. We dressed Margot in her best dress and waited quietly for the funeral home staff to come.

Margot was an outstanding person. Ann was an outstanding person. These twelve friends were outstanding and steadfast. I weep now as I recall.

—◦◦◦—

Caring for Caring Suggestion: Practice generosity.

44. Pleasant Surprises

Worry is a misuse of imagination.

—Dan Zadra

Florence and I went to church together, the First Presbyterian Church in Boonton, New Jersey, and we became friends. As we both aged, it was time for someone to get closer and check that she was all right living alone. Florence was ninety then.

I called or dropped by every day. She was a wonderful person, and I loved her very much.

One day in August she did not answer her phone, so I drove over there. When I walked in, I could hear that the TV was on, but she did not respond when I called out.

I searched the downstairs and finally found her lying on the floor in front of the TV, watching her beloved Mets.

She looked up and said, "It's cooler down here."

Ha!

—⁂—

Caring for Caring Suggestion: Trade worry for facts whenever you can.

45. Visits from Angels

Make yourself familiar with the angels, and behold them frequently
in spirit; for, without being seen, they are present with you.
                                        —St. Francis de Sales

The angels always visit, especially right near the end. As an elder moves spiritually closer to the time of leaving for the next world, we hold hands and sit quietly to await the angels.

We worked with Jeanne for only the last eight days of her life. However, during that period, we felt mesmerized by her genuine concern for everyone else in the house. We were included in this concern.

In addition to our services, Jeanne had two friends with her most of the time, and they provided excellent support as they catered to her every need. When she requested a glass of wine and oysters on the half shell, we briefly debated the advisability of such foods in her weakened condition. Then we all just looked at each other and agreed it was crucial to Jeanne's sense of dignity and justice. Using her glass of wine as a baton, she held forth for everyone's pleasure.

To her mind, life was fun, and she wanted to enjoy it down to the last minute. Kelly, my coworker, was with Jeanne on the night that the angels came. We usually do not speak in the moment when there is clear evidence that the angels are present, but Kelly could see a man standing at the head of the bed, and she asked Jeanne, "Who is that man?"

"Oh, that's my brother," Jeanne replied.

Jeanne went to join him shortly thereafter.

—◦◦◦—

Caring for Caring Suggestion: Keep your eye out for angels from this world—and the next.

46. Like It Is

*To truly laugh, you must be able to take
your pain, and play with it.*

—*Charlie Chaplin*

Jim Bob had been homeless as a child. The hard times he had gone through during the Depression sometimes made him cranky, and he was very careful with his money.

As we worked with Jim Bob, we learned that he would perseverate if his bank account statement was not correct and to the penny. Accounting is not my long suit, but another worker helped him, and they got along perfectly—well, almost perfectly—as they reviewed his bookkeeping together.

During shopping trips, Jim Bob was watchful of every penny. Under his guidance, we had to shop carefully and stretch every dollar to the limit.

He splurged one day and had us purchase fresh scallops from Roy Moore's on Bearskin Neck. After they were prepared and served, Jim Bob looked down mournfully at his plate and said, "These are the worst scallops I have ever eaten."

This was clearly meant to be taken as a reflection on the cook, not the scallops. My coworkers and I still laugh about it to this day.

Fortunately, Jim Bob also allowed us to joke with

him a bit about his penny-pinching ways. One day when my coworker Sylvia came to relieve me from my shift, I pointed out that Jim Bob's lower legs were swelling.

I said, "I am going to stay a few minutes, and we will give him a good massage." So Sylvia and I both got started and massaged both of Jim Bob's legs toward his heart.

Suddenly he said, "I am not going to pay the both of you!"

I replied, "Jim Bob, we are doing you a favor here." Then we all collapsed with laughter.

—⚬⚬⚬—

Caring for Caring Suggestion: Don't be afraid to tell it like it is—if laughter can lead the way.

47. Granting Wishes

The Lord Almighty grant us a peaceful
night and a perfect end. Amen
— *The Book of Common Prayer*

During the last three months of her life, we could tell that Charlotte was losing ground. We encouraged her to do whatever she wanted. She was a very wise woman, so she knew what was happening. She stated her wishes to us openly.

"I want to get a little table and chairs to set up on the front porch to invite people over for breakfast, one at a time. I have the chairs, but I need a table, which I don't intend to buy."

Charlotte went out walking with Ann, one of our team members, and you know it—on the side of the road was a round table with a sign that said Free. Ann walked Charlotte home and then went back for the table.

"We'll call it Henry's Place," said Charlotte. Henry was Charlotte's rescued cat. Charlotte began to issue her invitations, and she was joyously happy with the plan.

Shortly thereafter, she announced, "I would like to go to the Garden Club garden tour."

We advised her that she really needed a ride for this event, which involved moving from neighborhood to neighborhood. Another team member, Kris Higgins, secured two tickets and a map of the houses involved. She drove them as close to each garden as they could get without actually entering the garden. They had a wonderful time.

"I would like to go swimming at Front Beach," said Charlotte one hot day in July. She had a visitor at the time, but he wouldn't help, because he thought it was foolish for a person in Charlotte's frail state to attempt such a thing. Kris again came to the rescue. She drove Charlotte down to Front Beach.

The only space open was a handicapped space, and they didn't have a placard. However, Charlotte certainly qualified as handicapped, and Kris was set on her mission. She parked in the spot and slowly walked Charlotte to the water. Then she swam alongside until Charlotte had had enough. Later Kris said, "Charlotte's beauty outshone the sun."

After they returned very slowly to the car, they discovered a hundred-dollar parking ticket. However, when I brought the ticket to the parking clerk and explained the situation, he took it back.

In the early part of August, Charlotte announced that she wanted to walk to the water's edge on Back Beach at low tide.

"We can do that, Charlotte."

This time, we were able to park nearby. Then we walked with great difficulty down the ramp to the sand.

We ventured toward the water, and Charlotte set her goal: to make it out to the huge boulder that was only exposed at low tide, in order to grasp vigorously with both hands the seaweed that clung to the rock.

After achieving this aim, Charlotte was delighted, and we stayed quite a while because the boulder was in the shade of a huge tree that protected us from the sun.

One day we learned that Charlotte's family from California was coming to visit. I suggested to Charlotte that if she had any family jewelry, she might wish to give each person a love token. We went with great effort to the safety deposit box and retrieved what was needed, having left a note signed by Charlotte as to which items had been taken. When the family came, Charlotte was delighted to disperse her treasures to her loved ones.

Not long after that, Charlotte's legs weakened as we were walking through the kitchen. I steadied her and helped her to bed. As we went along, Charlotte asked me what was happening to her. After I got her to bed, I explained gently that her heart and kidneys and lungs had served her well for ninety-two years but that they were tired now and needed to wind up their mission.

Charlotte took a deep breath and closed her eyes. I sat quietly with her. After five minutes, Charlotte opened her eyes and told me she was ready for the rest of the journey.

The word got out among her many admirers, who

lined up outside the door. With Caring for Caring as maestro, they visited one at a time. Charlotte was exceedingly gracious and generous to all. This "living" wake served as her only tribute. Charlotte had requested that there be no memorial service or mention of herself in any way aside from a general announcement of her death from the pulpit of her church.

The night Charlotte died, Jane, the team member who was caring for Charlotte that evening, called me to say she had turned Charlotte only halfway. It is our custom to give bed-bound clients a full turn to protect their skin from breakdown. However, as Jane explained, it happened that Henry, Charlotte's cat, had hopped up on the bed and was stretched full out along Charlotte's spine.

"I knew that Charlotte would not want the cat disturbed, so we only went halfway over."

"Good for you, Jane," I said. Joy brought tears to my eyes from my gratitude at having such a sensitive coworker.

Jane called me later to say that Charlotte had died.

I went over right away. We left Henry where he was on Charlotte's back, and then I closed the door to have private time with Charlotte. We had often shared Compline, an evening service of prayer, with Charlotte reading one part and me the other. That evening I simply read both parts to Charlotte. We did not move Henry until the undertaker came to take Charlotte's body. After that, the beloved cat moved in with Charlotte's cousin.

Charlotte was all things to us, and we loved her beyond reason—honoring her wishes even when she could not express them.

—◦◦◦—

Caring for Caring Suggestion: Honor wishes.

Final Note

To listen, empathize, support, encourage, hold in my
prayers [is] to be a spiritual/emotional doula.
  —Joan Cannon Borton, Deep in the Familiar:
                        Four Life Rhythms

Recently I spent time with a woman who was dying. Her house was very busy, with phones ringing off the hook and family members and hospice volunteers preparing to move to the local hospice house.

In the midst of all this movement, I felt the need to simply sit with her and hold her hand. That's all I did—hold her hand—and because I knew her faith, every once in a while I would give her a little scripture to mull into her thoughts. She was unable to speak at that point, but each time I said a scripture verse, she would squeeze my hand lightly.

When the ambulance came, I made the sign of the cross on her forehead, kissed her, and thanked her for the four hours she had allowed me to spend with her. She thanked me back. This woman had touched my heart, and her inner voice was strong as she silently prepared to die.

As I drove home, I pondered people's two needs: first, to have the support to live independently as long as humanly possible, and then to have someone to sit and hold their hands as they are dying. And I committed myself again to the sacred roles that I wish to play for the rest of my life: to be a champion for the living and a doula for the dying.

Author Biography

Jane Edwards lives with her dog, Miss Pippi Longstocking, a rescued bichon frise. They are most compatible and live together softly. Jane loves to decorate, and they live in a whimsical, sun-filled apartment on the edge of Rockport, Massachusetts, near the beaches.

Miss Pippi loves the beach walks and window-shopping with Jane. Jane loves to read, especially first novels. She loves to cook and, in fact, has owned two catering businesses with partners. Jane gave up the catering businesses to work with the elderly.

Jane started her home care agency twenty-two years ago, and it has gone on successfully to a wide range of towns without advertising—just word of mouth.

Jane enjoys meditation and solitude.

Jane has cared lovingly for the elders for forty-five years. It has turned out to be her calling. This is her first written work of nonfiction.